SILENT VICTIMS IN THE UNITED NATIONS BUREAUCRACY

16 Décembre 1997

Chers les Haran,

Avec toutes mes amitiés et bons souvenirs.

A toi Bérengère, pour tout ton soutien moral et les bonnes conversations que nous partageons quand nous sommes ensemble.

Grosses bises.

Ta sœur Béatrice

SILENT VICTIMS IN THE UNITED NATIONS BUREAUCRACY

By

Béatrice K. Luvwefwa

AVON BOOKS

1 DOVEDALE STUDIOS
465 BATTERSEA PARK ROAD
LONDON SW11 4LR

Printed and bound in the U.K.

Avon Books

London

First Published 1997

ISBN 1 86033 291 9

ACKNOWLEDGEMENTS

Thanks

- to Elizabeth K. without whom this manuscript would not appear in its present form. She has provided invaluable advice in changing the order of the chapters, in clarifying some ideas and in making the manuscript more readable particularly for those who might not have time to plow through a long book;

- to Lynne L. for reading the manuscript over and correcting mistakes in English;

- to my three children: the oldest for retyping the manuscript; the two youngest for their sympathy and concern for me to find a job, believing that I am capable of using my skills;

- last but not least to my husband. Thanks for your love and patience and especially for having given me the opportunity for globetrotting with you.

This book is dedicated to all those silent victims who will identify themselves with it, and to my parents, who taught me to love all human beings because inside all of us there is blood and soul.

Synopsis

This manuscript recounts the pain of unemployed spouses living in the United Nations environment. The frustration that some spouses go through in not being able to find employment is often compounded with humiliation and discrimination. Spouses who seek employment do not know to whom to address themselves. The author has observed that the UN has enough qualified personnel to train people nationally so that they can become self-reliant. She hopes, however, through this manuscript to raise awareness in order to help reduce the self-interested and parochial behaviour which is undermining a system dedicated to non-political and international ideals.

Table of Contents

Foreword i

I. Introduction 1

II. Failure of the UN System to Help Spouses Find Jobs 7

III. Why are Spouses Silent Victims? 9

IV. How to Recognize Silent Victims in the United Nations Bureaucracy 11

V. Humiliation while Job-Hunting through Personnel Offices 19

VI. Discrimination 22

VII. Continuing Discrimination 25

VIII. Humiliation and Empty Promises while Attending Seminars ... 30

IX. Cheap Labour and Exploitation through Volunteer Work 36

X. Finding at Least a Short-Term Contract 43

XI. Expertise 47

It is somebody else who sees the depth of a wound in one's own back
Bantu Proverb

Foreword

The Organization of the United Nations was created in San Francisco at the end of the Second World War. The Charter was signed on 26 June 1945 and became effective on 24 October 1945. The Charter stated:

WE THE PEOPLES
OF THE UNITED NATIONS
DETERMINED

to save succeeding generations from the scourge of war, which twice in our lifetime has brought untold sorrow to mankind, and

to reaffirm faith in fundamental human rights, in the dignity and worth of the human person, in the equal rights of men and women and of nations large and small, and

to establish conditions under which justice and respect for the obligations arising from treaties and other sources of international law can be maintained, and

to promote social progress and better standards of life in larger freedom,

AND FOR THESE ENDS

to practice tolerance and live together in peace with one another as good neighbours, and

to unite our strength to maintain international peace and security, and

to ensure, by the acceptance of principles and the institution of methods, that armed force shall not be used, save in the common interest, and

to employ international machinery for the promotion of the economic and social advancement of all peoples,

HAVE RESOLVED TO
COMBINE OUR EFFORTS TO
ACCOMPLISH THESE AIMS

Accordingly, our respective Governments, through representatives assembled in the city of San Francisco, who have exhibited their full powers found to be in good and due form, have agreed to the present Charter of the United Nations and hereby establish an international organization to be known as the United Nations.

The purposes and principles of the Charter as well as the preceding quotation can be found in the Charter of the United Nations and Statute of the International Court of Justice published by the Office of Public Information of the United Nations in New York.

I am indebted to this organization which has kept its promises because there has not been a World War since 1945. Can anyone imagine the destructive potential, capable of wiping out the entire planet, of all the nuclear weaponry stocked by so many competing countries, big and small?

The United Nations has done a lot to contribute to global harmony, armament control, dispute settlement, free elections and much more. It has taken giant steps in alleviating the suffering of many people through the programmes, personnel and resources allocated by its member countries. The United Nations' successes and failures reflect the willingness of its members to help mankind cope with its problems in a changing social, political and economic environment.

The following chapters have nothing to do with the United Nations as an institution *per se*. We can all follow the praises to this organization in the official speeches on its recent fiftieth anniversary. That job is left to the real historians, professional journalists and politicians because they can do an in-depth analysis and evaluation of the organization.

The points of view and experiences, or rather frustrations, described in this manuscript are shared by some dependents, especially wives of civil servants working in the United Nations system. They are silent victims who do not know to whom to complain about the ill-treatment they are subjected to when job hunting. The purpose of this manuscript is not to create a negative survey on an innocent system with such a noble objective.

The names of some contributors are withheld, and the author alone accepts the blame for exposing the suffering of these dependents. Let us hope the spouses will understand and forgive the gloom on the faces of those who are supposed to cheer them up after a long day of listening to complaints about the financial cuts in the United Nations budget.

I. Introduction

The following reflections are neither fictitious nor pretentious, nor are they written with an intention of disparaging any United Nations or non-governmental organizations. They simply describe the experiences of some of the spouses of international civil servants.

The naming of some organizations is to demonstrate to those who like statistics that the facts are justifiable. Those organizations not mentioned are not exempt. It is because of lack of space and the fact that the purpose of the manuscript is not to investigate nor to judge, but rather to point out behaviour which is harmful.

The omission of people's names is to avoid pointing a finger at people whose behaviour might not reflect the principles of their institutions. If some individuals do not believe in the validity of these experiences, they can discuss them with colleagues or personnel officers over coffee-breaks.

Some spouses looking for jobs have many times applied for advertised posts or dropped off their curricula vitae at personnel offices, after being referred by acquaintances who do not always have proper information. Since it is always difficult for well-wishers to admit that they cannot help, they often send off their friends to try here or there on their own without the necessary guidance or background information.

In many instances these people make promises to help, thus building false hopes, and never get back in touch with the applicants. Sometimes one ends up dealing with unpleasant secretaries on the phone, who request all the details as to why one is calling. It is in the boss's interest to have the calls screened, but the secretaries do not have to make such inhuman and humiliating inquisitions.

In the few instances when I came upon pleasant secretaries, I thought I was not dealing with an international organization. I could not help thanking the women many times for their courtesy and willingness to take and relay the message for the boss. Now that secretaries are called "administrative assistants", it is very difficult to know with whom one is dealing. They easily feel offended when asked to take messages.

The biggest problem facing spouses looking for jobs, who phone to inquire about their applications reaching the right office, is the current United Nations budget cut. Everyone has become an expert on the subject. When posts were being advertised, one would often be reminded that there is no money for hiring new people.

I used to get a kick out of this United Nations "*mise en scène*" as a new style of make-believe or affirmative action: advertising for the sake of proving that the regulations or procedures are being followed.

The most painful experience is when one is told that the chances of getting the post are very good and then one discovers, after a long anxious waiting period, that it is not true. A few spouses go into depression. It takes a lot of encouragement for them to find self-esteem. Thank God it is typically a passing episode. There is no follow-up to measure the damage to these spouses, especially when the rejection is so frequent.

Personally I have been to UN personnel offices looking for work, sometimes responding to an advertisement or simply inquiring about organizations. You should avoid the latter approach unless you know someone who can take you and show you around. I have done volunteer work for one UN specialized agency and a few non-governmental agencies. I also attended seminars in the hope of getting somewhere or acquiring some useful skills, all without success. My own experiences have been echoed by other UN spouses I have met who followed the same itinerary and experienced similar disappointments.

At times I receive telephone calls at home from frustrated friends who have gone through rejections and disappointments. They are not all unemployed. There are those who work in the UN and who are not spouses of civil servants. The latter confront different kinds of problems and yet envy some of us at home. They may also think we are idle and enjoy a lot of free time.

"Aren't you lucky to stay at home?" say some. I wish that they could understand what those on the other side of the fence who do not work go through. If they regret working, then I tell them:

"Staying home is not heavenly. Many housewives don't choose that option. Besides, they don't enjoy coffee-breaks as do those who work outside their homes. There is always something to do and much more if you have children."

A few will acknowledge the amount of work in the house when they visit unemployed housewives once in a while. The discussions become the most emotional when they take place between involuntarily unemployed housewives themselves. Conversations can go as follows:

"I am very upset."

"Why?" I'll inquire.

"I hate to hear from those women who work that we housewives have a lot of spare time at home. They also tend to look down upon us as if we were stupid."

"Is that the first time you heard it?"

"No, but it is upsetting."

"Calm down and listen to me. We don't all stay home because we refuse to look for jobs. We just happen not to have the right connections. I have been to receptions where people ask only one question: 'Where do you work?' If that kind of environment disturbs you, just stay home and take care of yourself and the children. If nevertheless you decide to go and are asked to identify yourself by what you do, then proudly tell the other that you are a 'housewife'. There is nothing shameful about it."

In many cases people standing next to you, eager to brag with an "I work for this organization, how about you?" won't bother you. They'll smile at you as if you were an extra-terrestrial. One also receives the same treatment if asked the question on age. A few more years will earn you the comment: "I didn't know you were that old."

A very good friend of mine says it is her husband who answers for her when people inquire about her work. He always tells people: "She is the president of our big company." When the interlocutor continues and asks him what the name of the company is, he adds: "our family." She says people look perplexed.

After such a conversation, I try to sort out simple complaints from the reality of what many spouses go through. It is hard to accompany working spouses to work-related events because the conversations are always centred on their job. I only know of one man (that does not mean that there aren't many more) who used to refuse to talk about work outside the office, be it with those who worked with him (he was the head of a whole department) or with his family.

His example is worth following so that people can relax a bit. While at first it may not come easily, it will become a habit with time and will save those who work a lot of stress at home. They'll enjoy the benefits and lead better lives.

Many working women do not understand this. They have more time for coffee-breaks, to polish their nails and take lunch-breaks. Work at home does not have an end.

There is more to talk about in the next chapters. I hope at the end of these reflections I won't sound like Mrs. Mitchell during the Watergate episode. She was so eloquent about the whole affair that many people thought she knew more than her husband working at the office. The fact is one can't ignore what goes on when one's partner works.

As I stated in the Foreword, the elaboration of the manuscript concerns mostly my personal experience and recollections from conversations with friends in the past twelve years, during which I have been globe-trotting with my husband on his assignments. It does not reflect his opinion nor did I ask for it. His collaboration was not sought.

The contents of personal conversations which are painful are omitted. I have discussed the possibility of putting these reflections in writing one day with some friends (working and unemployed). A few volunteered to give quotations, which I refused. We agreed that it would be (a) encouraging and (b) interesting to express what some spouses go through and how they feel. Most of the time spouses suffer from people's ignorance and discrimination in certain agencies. Those who try to do volunteer work are exploited.

The forms to be filled in while job-hunting in the UN system are incriminating in some ways. While some qualified spouses find decent job opportunities, others do not. This will be explored in the appropriate chapter.

One argument used when one applies for an advertised post, when one has the luck to meet someone willing to listen, is that one is over-qualified for the post.

In a few cases I was told to take typing lessons so that I could find a job in the general service department. The contradictions in guiding and counselling applicants are revolting.

Another unbeatable argument is not having the required number of years of experience. How can one acquire it when one is not given a chance to start somewhere? It is as if those who hold posts were born into the system.

Most spouses, especially when husbands are frequently transferred, prefer to wait and raise children, if the couple has any, or until they both feel stable enough to invest in careers. In spite of disappointments with the official bureaucracy, evolving around the job market, volunteering for one or another organization is possible. This is done with a personal desire to find and pursue a career. The UN system has no office to guide or counsel spouses. When husbands are posted, there aren't any arrangements made at the country level to facilitate newly arriving spouses getting around the red tape and becoming quickly integrated into the local job market. Spouses may find themselves being bounced from one place to another without legal protection or job guarantees. By failing to protect UN spouses, the UN system turns them into silent victims.

II. Failure of the UN System to Help Spouses Find Jobs

The Universal Declaration of Human Rights was adopted by the General Assembly of the United Nations in 1948. Article 23 of this Declaration states:

(1) *Everyone has the right to work, to free choice of employment, to just and favourable conditions of work and to protection against unemployment.*

(2) *Everyone, without any discrimination, has the right to equal pay for equal work.*

(3) *Everyone who works has the right to just and favourable remuneration ensuring for herself/himself and her/his family an existence worthy of human dignity, and supplemented, if necessary, by other means of social protection.*

While the United Nations declared these rights nearly fifty years ago, it fails to protect these rights within its own family. Most of those who seek employment have no point of orientation and may even find themselves humiliated by the bureaucracy of the very institution for which their spouse is working. These silent victims do not know where to turn for counselling.

There are some agencies with circulars governing the recruitment and employment of spouses. There is still a big discrepancy between the good intentions of such circulars and their actual impact in obtaining employment for spouses.

While there are no statistics to evaluate the percentage of spouses willing to work while their partners are employed by the UN and its specialized agencies, it does not mean that the problem does not exist. There are many who try to find work and there are many reasons for doing so. Some want to pursue their careers. Some spouses had jobs where they came from. Others want to work to supplement their family income and to meet their financial needs. I want to stress that not all spouses want to work, nor am I suggesting that the UN and its agencies employ all those who do want to.

Spouses who follow their husbands may move to keep their families united, only to find that their skills are not being taken into account in the new duty station. This essay focuses on this particular group.

III. Why are Spouses Silent Victims?

These individuals have their own names. In certain countries spouses bear their husbands' names and in others they do not. When civil servants work for the UN and when a spouse obtains residency papers in their new duty station, she/he becomes *Spouse of. . .* thereby making independence and personal freedom in job-hunting a difficult process. UN Job Application forms require candidates to state the relationship between the applicant and a family member working for a UN organization. In France, one cannot work if one is a dependent of an international civil servant (spouse and children included). There is a work permit which applies to spouses of international civil servants who live in Switzerland and for which those spouses living over the border in France are not eligible.

Wherever they may be posted, spouses of civil servants who want to pursue their own careers have their hands tied. There are those who have special skills or aptitudes, including an invaluable awareness of their own culture. Such a spouse may be uniquely qualified to undertake a consultancy in her/his own country although those who are in a position to recruit consultants for such an assignment would favour imported experts who have previous UN working experience. Some spouses are willing to do short missions, but find themselves excluded by bureaucratic machinations.

The United Nations will continue to need civil servants. It also has to adapt to the needs of its employees. Does it wish to hire only single persons? If it hires married couples, is it willing to contribute to the benefits of united families? There are some men who move alone and leave their families behind. Is this situation beneficial to raising children, when both parents are fit to do the job? It is not too late to review the mechanisms. When spouses are happy and fulfilled, they contribute to the well-being of their families.

The lack of guidance and assistance for those who want to work is not the only source of unhappiness for UN spouses I have encountered. There are also other hidden causes which extends the circle of silent victims in the UN bureaucracy.

IV. How to Recognize Silent Victims in the United Nations Bureaucracy

After a whole decade of living in the Geneva region, being invited to dinners and other parties, the general impression is that many people are unhappy here. No personal interviews were conducted. By just chatting with people, their comments always tend to conform. The majority of those who work and who introduce themselves during parties cannot help but admit that feeling of unhappiness. An acquaintance told me that many people at her office become annoyed if they ask how she is doing and she replies " fine" with a big smile on her face, "You always smile as if you do not have problems", they say.

In some cases people take personal problems to the work place. The ones dealt with here are those encountered at the office and the ones people openly discuss when they gather together.

Why are some people unhappy? They are not all unemployed. Those who work make a nice living. Geneva and its surroundings are very safe. The Swiss people are very quiet and polite. The protection is the same for everyone, even more for diplomats. If one is being disturbed by noisy neighbours (including pets), just dial the right number. Your call will be answered. It is the same even for cooking spices whose smells may disturb the neighbours.

Unhappiness stems from different sources. Those who work are unhappy because their bosses give them shit, they tend to explain. It is not a complaint from just female employees. There are many men who put up with a lot from unkind and inhuman bosses. Once a man reaches the D1, D2 status or higher, he or she becomes a political figure. There are even those who acquire an autocratic power. Their working abilities are relayed to the ones down the ladder. They are the ones who write their speeches and reports. The boss's job is to give the speech or sign papers.

There are two major complaints from these employees: 1) there is no communication between bosses and employees; 2) there is no understanding of the workload, especially if one happens to have more than one boss. While the employee has to meet the deadline for the boss's work, he or she has work on his or her own as well.

This makes it very difficult for working people to relax when they meet outside offices. I have never been to a party where people just enjoyed themselves without ruminating about work. This general unhappiness with working conditions is not unique to one organization. It is reflected in many UN agencies.

When this essay was first drafted, it was known that spouses, including dependent children of those working for the UN system and diplomats, could not acquire federal work in Switzerland. The former could work in the UN organizations. The conditions were stated in the Foreword.

The acquisition of one international organization in Geneva completely changed the course of events. Thanks to the World Trade Organization, spouses and dependent children, if they reside in Switzerland, can obtain a work permit. Since Germany was keen to have the World Trade Organization on its soil, the Swiss authorities had to concede to one major demand from that organization: that their dependents find employment. Now the whole UN system can benefit from that favour.

One has to wait and see the application of the new package. It is an irony in one way because the Swiss are complaining about high unemployment especially in the French-speaking region, Geneva and its surroundings.

Now everyone will expect miracles from the Swiss authorities to provide employment to those dependents. How is the UN system itself dealing with its unemployed, most of them who are too old or who have been out of work for so long because of the complicated UN bureaucracy?

This brings us to the silent victims in the UN bureaucracy, the spouses. The children they raise still have a future, either finishing their school or moving out of the region to seek employment elsewhere. How about those who thought they married to live together "until death do us part?"

The budget of the UN does not seem to be increasing. The cuts have become a daily subject in newspapers as well as in conversations. While the majority of employees is lamenting its loss of posts, a few are only complaining about the negative effects of the cuts on projects or programmes with which they are involved. The largest portion of the UN budget is invested in the salaries of employees residing in developed countries, which is nothing compared to what is spent on projects in Third World countries. While the UN is not a profit-generating institution, the fat salaries of some employees are not proportional to their productivity. Some of them only count for promotional purposes.

The United Nations is an institution, a system in which many people from many countries with different cultural, educational and religious backgrounds work. It is not an institution where, to qualify for a post, one has to score high in moral or behavioural courses. That means that people who work in these organizations have as many faults and qualities as those who work in private institutions. Sometimes the quota business, which could be compared to affirmative action in the United States, only shows on the surface that there is a good transparency in the hiring system.

One day I was talking to a friend on the phone. The discussion was based on people's behaviour in general and of the UN personnel in particular. Why are some of them so pretentious? They seem to be wearing a tortoise's armour. When one meets them they give the impression that everything is great; but as one gets to know them on a personal basis, one discovers that they are carrying bombs inside them about to explode. Few talk positively of others. The friend added: "you can take a person out of the bush but you cannot take the bush out of a person."

People are so entrenched in their own cultures, it is very difficult not to reflect them in their working environment. One can look closely around the UN agencies. The inner circle of the Director General's advisors is not randomly selected.

Spouses who qualify for advertised posts should compete on the same basis as anyone else. There are those who do not want to work. Those willing to do it should be left alone to decide on how to juggle their responsibilities without any discrimination on the basis of the children or relationships.

Has the UN personnel noticed that the 20th century virus called divorce has started catching up with some of their colleagues? It happens for some after they obtain their pension. What has become of those "dear dependents" who sacrificed their own personal careers dutifully to follow their spouse around?

Even if the situation is not yet alarming, it is time to get something going for the spouses. There are some UN agencies where spouses get together for a bake sale or an informal walk. Why cannot there be some support groups?

There are other associations with such groups. Churches have meeting rooms. Yes, we all know they are moral entities. What prevents the UN system having support groups where the newcomers, especially dependents, could find some warmth? There are women's programmes in all these agencies. There are also departments which deal with social problems. Yes, initiatives can come from dependents themselves. Some of them do not come forward because they feel it will jeopardize their spouses' careers.

Three times we invited mixed groups (employed and unemployed) to dinner. There were some working women among the working men. The unemployed women approached the working ones asking "why do working women look down upon the housewives as if they were inferior?"

The working women were very humble. I knew them personally. I tried to defend them by changing the subject but my other guests did not want to listen and continued the attacks. I felt embarrassed. I later apologized to the working women. It becomes a problem when one invites people that one does not know very well.

Why and how can some groups exchange points of views to help? Some spouses think that they are personal failures. To feel fulfilled they have to work outside their homes. There are those who think that if they do not even complete one chore in the house during the daytime, they have not accomplished anything useful.

If a group has a positive attitude, it can raise the morale of its members. Once a friend and I became tired of job-hunting around the UN system. We decided to take a bus-ride to the outskirts of Geneva to talk to a lady who was just starting a non-profit centre for women.

We took buses in wrong directions because we were so excited and too much in a hurry to get going! We did not have time to study the maps to see in which direction we were supposed to be heading.

After a few stops, we asked other passengers and were told that we were going in the wrong direction. We jumped off and hopped on another bus in the opposite direction to discover we were wrong again. We kept checking the ticket to make sure it had not expired. By the time we reached the place to catch the train for Bardonnex[1], it was too late to continue. We took the bus back to Geneva. We were so excited about our adventure that we decided to repeat the experience. We accomplished nothing but felt great to spend some time wandering.

A few times we went together to inquire about job openings at some organizations. We felt less hurt if people tried to ridicule us while dropping off our CV at some agencies. Our sense of humour was so great and we took some of the people's attitudes with a lot of philosophy. It was a very positive experience.

Has anyone paid close attention to replies from job applications? Some of them are devastating. One has to be morally and psychologically strong to start again after receiving a few consecutive negative replies. I received a lot. Someone told me that if the envelope was heavy, it meant the answer inside was encouraging. I sent so many applications and never received one heavy envelope. At the end one starts guessing what could be inside. Either you get into the habit of throwing them away mechanically or you become curious to find out how each organization replies.

---

[1] A small locality on the outskirts of Geneva

Here are two letters not thrown away because the contents are very interesting. They are from two different systems: UN and a simple company. The candidates both had an advanced university degree and were applying for advertised posts. It meant that there was some kind of relation between the educational background and the advertised posts.

After careful appraisal of your application, I regret to inform you that your qualifications and professional experience have not reached the level required for this programme. May I suggest that you apply again in a few years when more experience has been obtained. Nevertheless, if you would like to participate in the UN Voluntary activities for developing countries, please write to the following address....[2]

The second letter is an answer from a company:

I am writing to thank you for your interest in the above-mentioned position. Without questioning the quality of your application, our choice has nevertheless been for candidates offering the qualities most closely conforming to the requirements of the post. Because of the quality of your candidature, we suggest that you re-apply for future positions we advertise that may interest you.[3]

---

[2] This has been freely translated from the original French which reads as follows: "*Après avoir soigneusement examiné votre demande, j'ai le regret de vous informer que vos qualifications et votre expérience professionelle ne sont pas* ***encore du niveau requis*** [emphasis added] *pour ce programme. Je me permets de vous suggérer de renouveler votre demande d'ici quelques années,* ***lorsque vous aurez acquis plus d'expérience*** [emphasis added]. *Néanmoins, si vous désirez participer aux activités des Volontaires des Nations Unies dans des pays en voie de dévéloppement, veuillez adresser votre requête à l'adresse suivante.....*"

[3] The original in French reads: "*Par la présente, nous vous remercions de l'intérêt que vous avez apporté à notre offre susmentionnée. Néanmoins, et sans que la valeur de votre dossier soit en cause, notre choix s'est porté sur des candidatures*

Both letters show that the candidates did not qualify for the advertised posts. It is not a question of being judgemental. The second letter shows some professionalism while the first one does not. It is arrogant. What guarantee will the applicant have to qualify for a post in that famous department after he or she has accumulated more experience and has acquired more knowledge? That kind of mocking behaviour towards the applicant and false hope have been going on not only in the UN system but in many other agencies as well.

This brings us back where the author started. When one is job-hunting and happens to be referred to some hopeful, well-wishing soul and you happen to entertain such a candidate, please be **humane** and do not promise much unless you know you can help. People look for connections because they work better in many instances nowadays than the official routes.

People in departments know where there are vacancies. Sometimes they are posted for transparency. Some posts are reserved for internal promotions. This is sometimes on the advertising forms. Looking for a job can be a traumatic and very trying experience. Some of you have gone through that experience. As a favour to those who are going through it now, you who have made it up there already, and since we do not know how, do not adopt the humiliating attitude.

The statement we hear most nowadays is: "finding a job is a matter of luck and coincidence. It is to be there at the right moment." I wish sincerely that some of us will be somewhere at the right moment.

Some spouses are tenacious despite lack of proper guidance, and they continue on their own to look for jobs. One has to have some self-esteem not to be let down by humiliation, discrimination and exploitation.

---

qui répondent plus précisement aux caractéristiques du poste à pourvoir. Toutefois, votre candidature présentant des éléments très intéressants, nous vous suggérons de nous écrire à nouveau si l'une ou l'autre de nos annonces était susceptible de vous intéresser."

V. Humiliation while Job-Hunting through Personnel Offices

The most complicated, powerful and sophisticated places in all those organizations are the Personnel Offices. Most staff-members are as cold as ice. They could be compared to advisors for foreign students at some universities, in that they are impersonal but at the same time, inquisitive. These characteristics also apply to the UN job application forms. Anyone who has already filled in a few for some organizations will know the sequence in answering the questions and the reactions to expect from interviewers.

The consensus is that those forms are *tedious* and *time-consuming*. All the questions do not carry the same weight. A very well-qualified person in that field told me that there are *three lines* which matter the most: a) the applicant's sex (male or female), do you have b) children, c) any relative working in a UN system and, if so, what is the relationship?

If one passes these crucial steps, there is a good chance that your credentials would be browsed through and considered afterwards. This can be understood if most of the application forms find their lodging in the garbage bins. There are too many to be taken seriously. For example, one is often asked to refer to the post's vacancy number to help identify the position one is applying for, although in truth this entry carries little weight.

At the beginning I thought that the personnel offices had big ovens to burn those cumbersome forms. Once I asked someone who had been in the UN system for a long time to help me type the job application form. The person told me not to include the passport photo required on the right corner of the form on the first page. She added that people would judge you from the photo without even reading another line. It was also true of hand-written forms. I thanked her.

The same thing applied as well to the question on stating what was relevant about yourself. Unless one had published some books or documents it was best to leave it blank. Wow! Was the information new! I have been describing all about my globe-trotting and how I lived in various places and mixed with all kinds of human beings, showing them that I could relate to the UN multi-cultural environment. No wonder I had never received replies to lots of my applications.

When we first arrived in the Geneva area, some people instructed me not to apply for work where my spouse worked. Fair enough, I thought. Anyway I wanted to take care of my baby and was not ready for job-hunting. Little did I know that it would become a nightmare to postpone too long. The number of years of experience would increase if one found a vacant position and staying home to raise a family would never have a space on the form.

I worked all the time while pregnant where we had been. So after our child was old enough to go to a nursery school, I decided to start looking for work.

I sent the curriculum vitae where I could, filled in forms in entrance halls where I could find them and left them with guards at receptions or just receptionists and answered ads on vacancies. A few replied stating that their organizations could not use my skills but thanked me anyway for showing interest in their activities. Some would kindly acknowledge the receipt of the letter clarifying that they would contact me in case my candidature was maintained for an eventual interview. These were the World Intellectual Property Organization (WIPO) and the World Council of Churches (WCC).

The ones which wrote that they "could not make best use of my skills," I kept in separate files, such as the World Health Organization (WHO) and the UN, at the Palais des Nations.

During that stage in the process of job-hunting, I came across an article from an American magazine. It stated that if one is looking for work, one should never take a simple no for an answer, especially if the reply is ambivalent. If one felt misunderstood, one should write to clarify the situation. Little did I know that that did not apply to UN agencies. An over-insistent attitude could become a source of discrimination.

VI. Discrimination

I pursued my quest with a specialised agency dealing with health problems. The letter I received said the organization "could not make best use of my skills". The words "best" and "skills" disturbed me. The letter was signed. The telephone number of the chief in question was on it. This time I wrote to him personally. I was excited because I knew I was corresponding with a person who had a name instead of bureaucratic machine.

The reply was no different from the previous one. That tickled me. All the people working in that organization were not medical doctors. I knew I could fit in somewhere because of two subjects I took at university. I phoned his office and talked to him. He sounded very nice and warm. He suggested that I make an appointment. Since he did not have time to discuss it with me, I should make it with another person, his assistant. The woman set the day and hour for the meeting.

On the day we scheduled the meeting, I arrived at the lady's office at 10.30am sharp. When I stepped into her office, I knew my soup would be full of little hot chilli peppers. She inquired about the job application form, the magical tool. I told her that she should have it since I sent it in with the Curriculum Vitae. She did not look for long before pulling it out of her drawer.

It is a matter of civility, I think, for them to have a little decency. Psychologically speaking, it is an abhorrence for a human to pretend not to acknowledge another in any such circumstances.

Anyway the lady tried to go over the job application forms and asked questions on why I was interested in working for the organization. Who will take care of the children? I answered her that I'd make the necessary arrangements for them. That question annoyed me during all interviews. Were men asked if they had children? Here is the Western world. People are implementing laws on equal opportunities for all, and, above all, a woman worries about what she will do with children if she finds work. This is discriminatory.

The lady continued her interrogation: "Are you interested in something else in the event that the post you applied for is not available?" I said yes, depending upon what it is. I could do work in grassroots programmes. Then the woman looked at me and added: "You know, we don't believe in qualified professionals who come here and pretend that they can do anything. Have you ever seen a doctor go and apply for a janitor's post and you believe that his intention would be to remain a janitor?" I did not understand what she was talking about. I told her that what I referred to was on the grounds of what I had studied at university and the fact that I held a teaching certificate. I could do some work in grassroots programmes in the field. Then she plainly came down to what was her biggest problem and stated: "Do you know that Africa has a regional office? Why don't you send your CV there if you want a job?"

I could not stand it any more and told her if she knew that there were lots of consultants who went to Africa sent by this organization's headquarters in Geneva who were not required to do work or research on African soil. I was thinking of an acquaintance I went to school with in the USA who was doing consulting work for that organization. She was called in from the States, her ticket paid for by the organization, to go to Africa. She never sent her CV to Africa. The woman's remark was so racist I could not believe what my ears were hearing.

I asked her to give back the CV she was holding so that I could send it to my continent. She refused on the grounds that she had to file it and could not give it back. I asked her what was the purpose. I knew such rules did not exist. If she wanted to fill her collection she had to make a copy and give back my papers. I asked her if she knew the time it took to fill in one of those forms. I did not want to waste any more time doing it. She made a copy; she handed it to me while she kept the original.

I was so defeated, so lost at sea that I did not see to whom to complain. I came back home and tried to make sense out of the ordeal.

Let me come back to why I went to the personnel office of this specialised agency in the first place knowing that only big doctors work there. The acquaintance I just mentioned above is European.

During one summer she stopped in Geneva as a tourist. She decided to collect some information and material for a paper she was writing at university in the States on some UN agencies. One person referred her to this organization. Since they were both from the same country, he told her to see one of their compatriots.

After an informal meeting, the man asked her if she was interested in doing consulting work for his department. The lady told me she didn't want to commit herself because of her studies and family, but agreed with the principle.

A few months after her return to the States she was contacted to come back to Geneva for a briefing for her first mission to the field in Africa. After the second mission she asked me if I had ever tried to send a CV to there. I answered yes, for volunteer work. She encouraged me to try again because we both had the same background. She added: "What more do I know about African cultures than you?" That is how I came to reintroduce the CV to the personnel office. I also knew about some vacancy possibilities at departmental level.

Later I learned that it was more useful to send applications to departments directly if one had connections so that it could be passed on, instead of to the personnel office.

VII. Continuing Discrimination

When one is determined to find a job, one keeps on trying despite all the pain and rejection. The deception at a UN specialised agency personnel office was not the only one. That one and the following are the extremes.

Another time I was referred to a community college near Geneva. After an unsuccessful search around the UN system, a lady suggested that I try outside Geneva. She had a friend who found a job teaching at this institution after a long try with international agencies. Why shouldn't I try? I had a few years of teaching experience. She gave me her friend's name.

The lady sounded enthusiastic and told me to make an appointment to discuss possibilities with a man in charge of the programme. The man's secretary set the time for 9:30am.

Not knowing where the place was located, I took off early enough from the house to find the town and the institution. I arrived ten minutes early at the entrance. I stopped at the reception and asked where the man's office was. The lady at the reception was nice and wanted to announce my arrival right away. I told her that I wanted to sit in the waiting room until it was time to go up.

"No," she said. She would check with the secretary because the man himself had gone up. If there was any objection, the secretary would say so. She phoned and I was told to go up. The man was ready to see me right away.

The secretary asked me to sit down while she let the man know that I was there. The boss came in with a cup of tea and a croissant in his hands. Apparently he was settling in his office to have breakfast.

I used to see secretaries at two UN specialised agencies do that. The first thing they did upon arrival at the office was to hang up their coat and rush to the cafeteria to have breakfast.

One lady used even to refuse any kind of conversation and told you right straight: "I do not like to talk to anyone until I have had my coffee. I do not take it at home."

That used to startle me. Here we are almost nine a.m. and some people are in a hurry to get to the office and go straight to have coffee when they should start work. What was amazing on top of that was that between 10 and 10:30 a.m. most of them go out again for a coffee break. Then, between 11:30 a.m. and 2 p.m., they go out for lunch which, in most cases, ends up at the cafeteria for a cup of coffee before heading back to the offices.

Let us not talk about the afternoon schedule and those stopping by offices who do not want to discuss anything in the office but would prefer the cafeteria environment.

The interviewer settled himself in a chair next to the secretary. By his look I knew he was up to something unpleasant. At least the CV was out in front of him. He greeted me by my husband's name. Incredible, I thought, because usually people I saw on interviews could not care less. Then he saw where I was born. The name of the country had changed as had a few others in the Third World. I gave him credit for remembering the old name. At least he knew his history and geography.

This brings up a problem I had already dealt with in the UN system while applying for jobs. There are three lines to state your nationality, at present and at birth, and a last inquiry on whether you are in the process of changing your latest nationality.

I no longer have the nationality I did at birth, but it is the one my interviewers always refer to. Do not ask me why. That is what the man started with.

His questions were very personal. Why was I living in France? I thought this was none of his business. To be polite I told him why. I did not choose my residence because I was a married woman. I just accepted my husband's choice. I guessed if he was a spy he might as well satisfy his curiosity because I had nothing to hide. Then he went on and asked why I was interested in this institution with the type of diplomas that I earned from university. I did not have a doctorate degree.

Glancing at the secretary, the man took more courage and pleasure because I stopped answering his questions. I did not deserve the humiliation he was pouring over me. I lost my patience and told myself to speak up. I had nothing to lose. The man did not deserve my courtesy. I wanted to show him that I was not an insect but a human being with emotions. I did not want him to do the same thing to another person after me.

Then I looked straight up at him with dignity and asked him if I lied to him about my educational background and working experience. I had also explained at the beginning of the interview how somebody sent me to see him. I knew from the person who sent me there that the lady who referred me to that institution did not have a doctorate either. She was still working there. Why was he taking such a fiendish pleasure in acting the way he was? Finally I told him to return the CV.

He suddenly looked embarrassed. He asked me if I knew a certain man at a UN agency whose name he gave me. He could refer me to him because I had already worked for the organization. I told him I could return there on my own since I did not need his help or influence. I was trembling with indignation and about to cry. I held my tears back, escaped from his office and ran quickly down the stairs. I went to where I had parked the car. I was very confused and wondered what to do next. Should I phone my friend and tell her how disastrous the interview turned out to be? No. I did not want to make her suffer.

I decided to drive to Geneva anyway and maybe call my husband. However I decided against this because I was worried I might break down crying. My chest hurt and my heart was pounding very hard. I just drove around the Palais des Nations and made a turn and headed back home.

I also tried to send the CV to the Palais itself. I was turned down for two reasons: a) I was too qualified for the advertised posts, b) I could not be hired as a consultant because they relied on the roster to send people to the field. Many applications for specific vacancies remained unanswered. I cannot recall a single UN agency in Geneva to which I did not apply.

Once a lady at another UN agency specialising in work matters asked me: "What brought you to this department of this organization? We do not need people with your experience." After a little inquiry I learned that she herself did not even have the right qualifications to work there. It is sometimes a matter of who one knows and when one gets there. I gave up fighting with narrow-minded people for good.

One day I was having a discussion with a lady who once worked for a UN agency as secretary. She quit to raise her children. For financial reasons, she decided to go back where she used to work. After all the years of being out of work and changes in the computerised system, she managed to find a post where she used to work. She once complained herself how she had to start from scratch again due to all the changes in her workplace and the years she had spent not working.

During our discussion, I brought up the doubtful hiring methods used in many UN organizations. I knew that she had not gone to secretarial schools either. The discussion was just based on facts and techniques. The lady was so defensive she even started talking about some cases I knew well. I pointed out to her that I was not going to accuse people in the UN Court of Justice in the Hague. There are many secretaries hired as bilingual but who nevertheless appear to have problems speaking a second language. The lady could not even convince me there were exceptions. There is a proverb which says: "It is hard to tell and accept the truth because it always hurts."

There were some friends who suggested that I learn how to type. They said that it would be easier to find a job as a secretary.

One day, while discussing this with a very qualified acquaintance who had worked in the UN system until retirement, I mentioned what I had been advised. She blasted at me saying: "Would they give that advice to a Western woman in your situation? I have known many people in the UN without the right training who hold responsible posts because of the colour of their skin. Do not humiliate yourself." I told her that I was not trying to do so.

I was sceptical about the secretarial training for a few reasons: 1) I was married. Most Third World women secretaries I came across were either single, widowed or divorced, only a few were married; 2) by the time I would qualify, the criterion for selection would have changed. Besides, I would never be able to roll my " r's " like a French person nor have a nasal accent like the English. I would not put any financial burden on my husband's salary because we needed to put the children through school. How was I going to apply on paper? After the experience with the lady at the personnel office of a UN specialised agency dealing with health, I would rather apply for a job as an honest and a convinced janitor.

A woman I know gave up her university training to become a secretary. One has to see who she is. She also comes from a powerful country. For some of us the quota business is screened with magnifying glasses.

By lack of a proper office to guide spouses in what steps to take and where to go on a job-search, one can keep accumulating rejection and even humiliation by following the advice of well-wishers.

VIII. Humiliation and Empty Promises while Attending Seminars

Geneva, the city of Calvin, has the most UN agencies (specialised included) and non-governmental agencies (accredited to or with no special status to the UN system) of all the cities in the world.

Switzerland is not a UN member itself but is the second UN centre after New York City. It even beats New York City in the number of annual conferences. With some connections one can be aware of some conferences' importance. Hence one can obtain an official badge from a participating agency and attend. I am not talking about big conferences where one gets hired and paid.

If one is job-hunting, a well-wishing soul would suggest that one attends some conferences because one can make contacts with interesting delegates outside the usual UN system. In that case one has to be bold enough to strike up conversations with strangers, especially if they are diplomats.

These conferences are impressive first of all by the number of people and second by the amount of paper consumed. Of the ones I attended, the list of people was printed out on a daily basis because some did not come to the first session due to travel problems, etc. After three conferences and two seminars, I collected enough material to read for the rest of my life. The library at the Palais des Nations in itself is very famous for its contents in documentation.

During one Non-Governmental Organization (NGO) conference, an acquaintance invited two of us, both housewives, to attend and see if we could make some personal connections. We received badges under his NGO. There was an official lady who came from a Third World country. Hence we made a team of four people.

The two housewives became secretaries taking notes for the person in charge of the group. Our leader had to refer to others' discussions in his own exposé. It annoyed us a lot because that prevented us from speaking on a personal basis with other delegates.

During break-time we put our notes together and did not always agree on the content. The conference lasted four days. I did manage to talk to an American delegate from Los Angeles, California. We exchanged Christmas greetings for a while.

The most touching meeting was the one with an Italian veteran. His speech on why the world should give up war had a long-lasting impact on me. I had two boys who could one day be drawn into fighting. The man painted all the atrocities of war as he had lived them himself. I asked for a copy of his speech, which he declined to give, but we exchanged addresses and Christmas greetings. The conference ended without any connections jobwise.

One can also find internships, most of the time without pay. There are seminars as well. A woman wanting to help once referred a young lady and myself to the touring section of the UN Palais des Nations to attend a seminar training people to become guides.

We both had university diplomas: she had a degree in law and I had a higher university diploma. "Why not?" we told her. "We have been job-hunting for a long time." Being guides, we could at least represent our respective countries.

I was thrilled because an acquaintance who used to work as a touring guide in New York City said she wore her national costume. That would be fantastic even if I didn't know what my national costume would be; I'd been leading an international life for the past twelve years. We phoned the person in charge and made appointments for interviews. They went well. The person told us the right procedure to follow and how to register.

The person did not point out the fact that the UN made a deal with the Swiss authorities to give priority in hiring Swiss students who were in their senior year for guided tours during summer.

Anyway, I was eager to start the seminar. It was after the seminar that we found out about the preferential hiring. I was happy to find any job as long as it involved outside activities for which I could earn a living on my own.

The acquaintance and I went on a guided tour conducted by a young lady. She wore a UN uniform, not a national outfit. That gave me a good kick. One had to really be in shape to wear that uniform because it looked so sharp and standardised. We came across more guides, male and female, all with the same tailored uniform.

All the candidates to participate in the seminar met in the waiting room of the new wing of the Palais des Nations, from where the guided tours start. The group was quite large. Then we were led to the old wing which used to house the League of Nations.

The conference lasted a few days. Speakers came from everywhere and not only from the Palais but from UN specialised agencies as well. They covered all topics: historical backgrounds, recent events including hot topics, such as diplomatic courtesies in seating representatives from antagonistic countries during conferences.

Manuscripts on guided tours were to be memorised line by line, not skipping or changing sequence within the paragraph. I knew from the way the person in charge was emphasizing the fact that it would be the same during examinations time. We went on tours with guides, visited the halls according to the described itinerary.

The inside of the Palais des Nations, not to mention the halls and conference rooms, is very impressive. There are many gifts offered by member countries and pieces of art by famous painters and incredible architecture.

One day during lunch my friend and I decided to rehearse our new skills and make sure our memorised details on guided tours would satisfy our examiners. We went back to the new wing.

While walking in the long hall connecting both wings, we came across some Africans going to lunch. We both recognised one official we met separately at the International Labour Office. We were referred to him to make connections. He remembered neither one of us. We warmly greeted the man singling him out by name. We each reminded him why we knew his name. He seemed very pleased and asked us what we were doing at the Palais des Nations. We told him that we were being trained to become guides. He then replied: "Bonne chance, mes filles. Que Dieu vous protège," meaning: "Good luck my daughters. May God bless you." After they left, my friend and I started laughing. She said: "It is only Africans who trust God in these organizations."

The examination date was set on a Saturday following the seminar in January, early in the morning. The person responsible for the section for guided tours supervised it. The person was autocratic but courteous. Even during the seminar one got the impression that all the Palais belonged to this person. We were told, as if we were high school students, that cheating was not tolerated. I thought the warning to be childish because all those young people looked mature enough to not do such a thing. Afterwards I learned that there had been some precedents. Later we learned from gossip that one woman succeeded in seducing a guy and cheated.

Our boss stood guard over the examinees. The questions came from the papers we were given during the seminar and had to be answered textually. A few days later, we set up appointments to go over the results. It was also part of an interview. A second person from the personnel department came to assist the person in charge of the guide's section to interrogate the candidates.

For the first time I noticed that the one responsible was playing games with us. She put on such airs I felt like walking out on both of them. She had the text in front of her and wanted it to be repeated line after line and would become angry and excited when one did not follow even the punctuation.

To ease the tension, the person from the personnel office would intervene and ask questions on the UN system and the specialised agencies. The lady was using a sarcasm which did not show any professionalism.

At the end of the interview they asked me to call back to find out the final decision. One could sense that it was just a matter of procedure; the real decision had already been made. Before leaving the Palais I stopped by a telephone to inquire the second examiner's name and phone number. The reason I wanted to know more about him was that he had made unpleasant remarks. One of them was that guides should restrain themselves from talking too much during the tours. Some people from specific countries were known to be talkative. The second examiner kept on glancing at the person in charge of the selection.

Upon arriving home I rang him up. He was back in his office. I introduced myself since we just met each other not long ago. He remembered who I was. I asked him if the way I was being interviewed seemed ethical. He replied he knew what I was referring to and added that the other examiner had all my papers in the office and was aware of my educational background. He seemed very warm then and honest. He informed me about the actual intentions of the seminar and how there was an agreement with the Swiss authorities over hiring students in their senior year for the summer job. Therefore if I was seriously looking for a job, not to let myself be humiliated but look elsewhere. We would not be hired even if we passed the test.

By this time I was also talking about my other friend. I phoned the latter to inform her. She said she had the same experience during the interview and almost broke into tears. Her interview was a fiasco!

"What was new?" I asked myself. The litany stayed the same in the UN system: priority to this quota business at the country level, marital status, rosters for consultancies. All those UN terminologies had already invaded my little brain. The only option left seemed to turn the wheels in a new direction and close the chapter on guided tours, and keep going.

Since a paying job was not within my limits and some friends kept on suggesting volunteer work, which they explained would lead to job opportunities, I decided to give this a try. What people failed to stress was that the experience was painful because some spouses were exploited. One is not only exploited by little organizations (NGOs), but one can encounter the same attitude within UN agencies as well.

IX. Cheap Labour and Exploitation Through Volunteer Work

Volunteer work is readily available and plentiful for those spouses who want to spend some time out of their homes. It can be done at either a non-governmental or a UN organization. A few offer unpaid internships. There is encouragement when one embarks on this adventure. "Volunteering is helpful in acquiring some experience, meeting interesting people and making useful contacts. It can sometimes lead somewhere." "Why not?" one thinks. Anyway looking at the four walls in one's home is no more fun than going out. With that kind of enthusiasm the optimist sets off to investigate.

There is always someone who has a little project put off because of too much accumulated work in a non-governmental or UN agency. There is not enough money because some member countries are not sending in their contributions to hire new staff members for some UN and specialised agencies. It seems odd that there are plenty of funds to finance staff members' missions while at the same time unpaid volunteers are used to take care of the backload of work which the same staff members leave behind.

A lady from an NGO I worked with attended meetings most of the time. When she came back to her office, the first thing she did was to stand in front of a mirror to admire herself and check her looks. The other volunteer and I used to laugh a lot.

Our primary duty consisted in answering her correspondence, then filing documents and finally writing small project documents to apply for and justify new funds. A lot of volunteers take their responsibilities seriously, and why not, when some of the work to be done could help others? That is the case with some NGOs, which work to promote women's rights projects or just to defend human rights in general.

A friend and myself found ourselves at an all-women's NGO in Geneva. We did not have the same educational backgrounds but could both contribute in our fields. The major problem we encountered was the absence of the woman we were supposed to help. We had to make special appointments to discuss whatever we were doing.

Commuting from a neighbouring country did not help. It meant going in on days we did not plan to. Neither one of us was receiving any money to pay for the gas we were using driving our personal cars to that office.

The lady in charge of volunteers told us that the organization was looking into making volunteer work more appealing because they were losing good help by not providing any incentive. Some quit just a few days after they joined. One incentive could be to give a small amount of money for transport.

The section of town where the NGO was located had few parking places available. It took us little time to receive parking tickets.

Thinking that these ladies would be understanding enough to pay for a twenty Swiss franc parking penalty, we presented the tickets to the lady who hired us. She just looked and simply said how sorry she was and that she could not help. We decided to bring the tickets to our husbands' attention and asked them to pay. I told mine: "Here is a parking ticket. When other wives bring pay checks, the only thing I can add to your budget is another expense." We laughed and he paid for it.

It was difficult to park near the office because, even if one found a parking meter, one would never beat the Swiss police or Swiss citizens' vigilance. After one minute of expiry, one would need Superman's flying speed to beat the ones who put tickets on the cars.

That is how my friend and I decided to look somewhere else after we finished the work we were asked to do.

A personal incident tipped me off to the general attitude at that NGO. One day the lady in charge of volunteer management gave me some work. As usual, it basically consisted of filing her correspondence. Remember what a French proverb says: "Il n'y a pas de sots métiers. Il n'y a que de sottes gens," meaning literally, "there aren't any stupid jobs. There are only stupid people." There was such a backlog I could not believe my eyes. The sight of it was enough to discourage the enthusiasm of any willing soul.

Since the filing took place in the lady's office, we started chatting. I asked her at one point if she would do what she gave me to do if she happened to be a volunteer. She looked up right at me and said: "No way would I do it free." I did not say another word. She might not have noticed but my pace slowed down. I put the rest of her correspondence together and told her that I had to leave. I had something else to do.

I never set foot back there to do volunteer work. Here is a lady who felt enthusiastic to volunteers'work, who wanted to suggest an incentive so that they could stay and at the same time felt indignant working without pay. It showed that those ladies did not have any regard for the others doing volunteer work. I went back to that office only one more time, to explain some terms, such as "per diem," (daily allowance) which I used in the project document and with which the lady was unfamiliar.

My friend and I never received a simple thank you for our useful work, not that we expected it, but because we did some useful work for them. The last time I saw the lady I worked with was at the airport heading off to one of her favourite meetings. She was shocked that I recognised her. She said she didn't recognise me because I had put on some weight, which wasn't true. She excused herself saying that she didn't spend enough time with me while working at her office. I should give her a call upon her return from Provence and she promised to improve her attitude. I said yes, but never bothered getting in touch.

There are other NGOs where, in spite of lack of funds, the people in charge make an effort to be courteous. There was another all-women's NGO I worked for. The lady in charge told me she could help with gas, but never did, although she behaved correctly.

I worked there for a month. The person responsible for the programme told me there could be some opening in my field with the arrival of the new person. It became too expensive to commute, so I gave up. The work was interesting, though, because one had the opportunity to read a lot. The NGO was affiliated with the UN and published its own articles and magazines. It sponsored internships for young women from around the world for a year.

Promises to help people sometimes become a way of not hurting feelings or avoiding disappointment. In the end those looking for work start to discover that these promises do not lead anywhere and give up.

One has to be emotionally sound to face the reality and not to take it as a personal rejection. Promises leave one disillusioned and in limbo.

The longest volunteer post I held was at a UN specialised agency dealing with health. It lasted for six months. A good-hearted woman sent me there. After looking at the curriculum vitae, she advised me to give it a try.

The man who hired me was very courteous and nice. He said he would be retiring in one or two years but gave me enough encouragement to stay. He asked me to help a lady in his department.

The work consisted of selecting clippings from major newspapers and articles sent in by regional offices to be published in one of their magazines. It was voluntary to start with but there was a good chance that the department would need my help and pay for it later. Anyway, with the arrival of the new director, things could work out better, the man added.

I was told not to worry about my personal security. Even if I received no salary, I was covered by insurance while still working on the agency compound. This meant that any injury incurred during those hours, even costs for hospitalisation, would be totally covered.

This sounded very funny. What hadn't I heard so far in this volunteer business? My major concern was that I did not live in Geneva and was commuting from a neighbouring country. What if something happened while driving to my safe haven where I was covered? Or what if I fell down where I parked the car before getting to the entrance of the building?

Working for six months meant I could not avoid going there in winter as well. I did not ask the man. I did my best not to fall walking on the ice outside the building. I became a great driver, never racing on the road to get to Geneva. It was not easy to avoid, because there were many nervous drivers on the road. Assuming they had decent jobs and insurance, I kept my pace. I took the unpaid job.

Most people in the department were nice. The one I had to work closely with seemed very moody but I tried to cope with it. They invited me to the weekly meetings. The director first told the group what he had done in the past week, whom he had met and what he had discussed. I thought that was kind of neat. The meetings in themselves were informal but instructive. Then everyone was asked to share what he or she had to say or had done.

Then the new director came. There was an overlapping period during which the former chief briefed the new one on the department. All the staff members met the new director on a personal basis to discuss what they were doing. I too was asked to go and do the same. After our discussion, the new director told me that the department could use my help in a more constructive way. I could help in screening and reviewing movies from Third World countries before the organization uses them for official purposes. There had been some complaints about lack of taste. The point of view of a person from the Third World could help prevent that kind of indignation. Some countries said the raw information as it was presented in the films was demeaning and offensive to those who allowed those films to be made. Such films were sent as didactic material and not for propaganda.

Wow! Was I happy at last to feel useful in my volunteer venture! I went back to doing what I was hired for while waiting for the new assignment. I waited and waited. Nothing changed. I thought I should give the new chief some time. Still nothing happened for two months.

One day I was sent to the AIDS library to help organise the material which was piling up. The library could not keep up with the incoming articles and books. Two women were already working there, one as a secretary from the Third World and the other from the Middle East waiting for a contract. The latter needed help.

When I arrived she started acting like my boss. She found herself a corner and hid there. She was being paid and I was not. When I went back to the department which sent me to the AIDS library I asked the people what kind of arrangements they had made on my behalf. They told me I was there as a volunteer (working under the same conditions, without pay). I was mad. Then I asked them if they knew that there was a vacant post at the library. Why didn't they tell me about it, especially since I had done some work and had experience as a librarian for two years. I was stupid. It was on that background that they sent me there in the first place, I thought afterwards. I could at least have applied. I told them that I was looking for a paying job when I first went to them. Why did they start trading me off without my consent as if I was merchandise?

I sought advice from a few friends, including the one who sent me there. Anyway I had kept her informed on these people's behaviour. They told me not to quit while I was still angry. Didn't the department talk about screening movies? Maybe the project would materialise one day. If I wanted to distance myself because I felt hurt, I could at least write to the new director saying that I was taking two weeks off. I had already been there six months. There was a good chance that the new director would respond. Then I could sense what her future intentions were.

I wrote to the new director, as I was told, and also wrote to the former director because he was still around, just to cover myself. I didn't want to be accused of running away. I also accepted the volunteer work for recommendations for a potential post. Staying home to raise children is not a credential when filling in job applications. So I decided to follow the advice.

The day before I took both letters in, I arrived early as usual. The former boss's secretary was in the office. We exchanged the ritual greetings. She looked up at me and said: "Vous êtes vraiment résignée?" (meaning: you have really given up?). Her mocking and sarcastic tone of voice made me want to say something but I just looked at her and walked out of the room.

The next day I handed in the letter and quit.

I called my friends and told them that their organization was not a charity. The lady at the AIDS library signed her contract while I was still volunteering. What a big surprise it was later to see her give a seminar to technical officers being briefed for the field. I could not believe my ears and eyes.

Neither the departing nor the new director acknowledged my letter. After six months I left the organization.

When official bureaucracy does not work, one can rely upon some unofficial acquaintances. It is a question of whom one knows.

X. Finding At Least a Short-Term Contract

The preceding experiences did not prevent me from obtaining a few short contracts with the same agencies which refused to consider my job applications before. The connection system finally worked. Someone I knew had a friend who was in charge of short consultancies in one organization. I was very reluctant to go at first because I did not think it would be of any use. I was qualified for the work. The department accepted me, thanks to the recommendation given by the person in charge.

At another organization, it was one of the people on the hiring committee who stubbornly defended my application. I had already done the work they were advertising, while the man some of them favoured had not. Besides, the person in favour of my CV told them that the rival applicant was looking for a prestigious post and would not accept their offer for a few reasons: 1) the work was too boring, manual and of low profile; 2) the salary was very low (I accepted it myself especially for future reference in case I applied for better posts); 3) it was a short-term contract and did not lead anywhere. Maybe his contract could be renewed, but the job description did not carry any message like that.

Anyway, I was given the job. Wow! What a nice feeling to earn a little money to buy the family a few surprises and replace some household items which were in bad shape. My contract ended and was not renewed because the work was done as described.

At another UN specialised agency I had to go on three missions in the field. The briefing was very short. I met the people with whom I travelled. The explanation of my duties during the mission was unclear. Nobody had time to go into detail. They all looked so frantic! It was only upon returning to headquarters to write the report on the mission that I learned that my job consisted of filling the information from the country in the provided space. The document was a prototype. I was going to a lot of trouble writing an explanatory report.

It was worse in the country. The experts from Geneva were very grouchy and unfriendly. Some were critical of everything and found people slow and disorganised. I was strolling behind and observing. Considering the lack of equipment I thought the people in the field were doing a decent job.

I concentrated on taking notes during the conferences, knowing that the man I accompanied was not going to do such low-skilled work. He was constantly depending on mine. His interest was just in the financial figures. Most of the time I missed lunches and official receptions because I had to draft the report for the next day or meeting.

At the end of the day the man in charge of our group would be making unpleasant comments in the lobby if he found me chatting with the national delegates. I had no problem conversing with the nationals because I am a Third World person myself. I was trying to find out more about their daily life. They had the same problems as my own countrymen. I felt the leader of our group was rather jealous and thought I was aligning myself with these people. He finally came out with it at the end. During the two or three days that the conference lasted, the atmosphere was very tense. Then the experts left. I remained in the country a week or so longer to collect more data and information. My working conditions became more human.

During one mission I could not take the insulting behaviour of one expert towards the nationals any longer and told him off. He became so enraged that he wrote a confidential note when he returned to Geneva. He told his department not to send me as a consultant any more. He made two crucial mistakes: 1) he should have filled out the evaluation form and evaluated my professional capacities, which he did not; then he could have added a note to explain why I was not fit for consultancies; 2) he did not know that confidentiality is temptation to the curious. One acquaintance told me: " If you want a complaint to go around faster and be read by many people send it marked CONFIDENTIAL."

When I learned about what he wrote, I went to see him. He tried to justify his attitude. He said he would make some arrangements with others to see if they could also still use my help. I just thanked him and told him that I had learnt a lot from him during the two missions. I had a family and did not want to have a depression. I could not care less for another contract. I accepted the previous two because I needed some experience for the CV. I had another consultancy in that organization, but under someone else who knew well my previous misadventure and disappointment with one of his colleagues. He told me that he also knew of the confidential letter.

After all these reflections on the UN system and its related organizations concerning its failings to integrate and guide spouses who are willing to find employment, the author dares suggest a few principles. The UN budget is shrinking and member countries are becoming increasingly reluctant to pour huge sums into a system which they consider to be wasteful.

The following chapter on expertise may have nothing to do with spouses' disappointments in job-hunting. Rather it is based on my own perspective on what is going on, despite the fact that I have not been directly involved with the concerned people or organizations. The media has made it easy to see, through television or newspapers, what is happening around the world. The following observations and proposals are inspired by my own personal field experiences, combined with my own reading of events as portrayed in the media. Whilst the experts may not agree with my principles, I am convinced that they are worth discussing, for the majority of people who have not had the opportunity to live those experiences first-hand.

Since 1945 when the UN was founded, many things have changed. There are still wars among certain countries, but the economic challenge has created another problem. Migration is becoming a major concern for both industrialised and developing countries.

How can the UN system help people find dignity and meet their basic needs when the effective transfer of technology between the rich North and the poor South is not a dream for tomorrow? How can it best make use of the expertise of its employees?

XI. EXPERTISE

There is no dispute over the fact that there are many civil servants in the UN organizations with specialised skills. Before talking about these experts, let me tell you a short story.

During the summer of 1987, our family decided to go on vacation and have a good time. To do so we wanted to try to do it *à la carte*, meaning we would not make any reservations. We would travel throughout England to Scotland and make reservations along the way. There would be tourist and information centres on the highways. We would stop and call some places.

It turned out to be a great idea. We got a lot of help from people working there who suggested the best B&B (bed and breakfast). It was the first time I had heard that word. They would say things on the phone like: " Here come some B&Bs". The experience was worth trying.

At one B&B there was a couple who happened to be the owners. The husband had retired from his work and had been travelling ever since. He even made it to China. There he learned some recipes, his favourite being chicken. He volunteered to make it for us.

The chicken was sliced into thin pieces. He added a very pink sauce (which did not taste like any Chinese sauce I had ever had in any Chinese restaurant before). He told as we left that he was an engineer.

While I tried to enjoy his exquisite chicken *à la chinoise*, I kept glancing anxiously at my husband and the children. I wondered if we would be alive after this meal. If we all died, who would know we had ever stayed there or what had killed us?

After we retired to our quarters, I teased my husband, making sure the children did not hear what I said. I did not want them to be alarmed and panicky. I whispered: “Are you sure the engineer knew his ingredients? The chicken did not taste Chinese at all.” We both laughed and he added: “He is an expert on Chinese food. Let us hope he did not put in some wrong ingredients.”

There is always a problem in exporting expertise. The UN experts are not the first ones. Before them were the colonialists. They became experts in all fields assuming the indigenous people did not have any knowledge of what was around them. Nowadays many nationals have the same training as foreign experts, but are always bypassed by the latter when it comes to dealing with problems affecting a country, people or culture. Here are two examples to illustrate the preceding observation.

A person I have known for a long time, working for a UN specialised agency, went on two missions to West Africa. In the group there was a lady from a Nordic country. Part of her mission consisted of looking into excision (female circumcision), how and why it was performed.

Being a woman nowadays, we all feel concerned about the practice and want to find a solution to stop what many societies call a barbaric act.

The woman was the only female among the male experts, most of them Western like herself. According to the informant, our lady, being so obsessed about her crusade on excision, would not listen to any warning. All her interventions during meetings with male nationals were on excision, the subject being out of the context of what was being discussed. Nobody could restrain her.

She spoke neither the national language nor knew the culture. If she knew one of the two, culture or language, she would have known that her subject and concerns could have earned her credit had she discussed the subject with the target group: women themselves. Maybe the lady learned about the hot subject of the mutilation of women’s genitals in school or from newspapers.

The women in the village are the ones who live with the scars. They were not even sought out or encouraged to participate. The men whose opinion is being sought could be in favour of the practice, which seems to be the case.

There have been some trials on excision in France, inv both parents or just excision done with relatives' complicity. Calling for these people to stand trial did not mean that little girls could not be excised when they are taken back to their countries on vacation. In some cases, real parents are not aware of what is being done to their children.

Many Westerners talk about African women's submission. To respect one person regardless of who he or she is, parent or husband, may not be a sign of total submission. Many women lead very independent lives when one digs deeper into the cultures.

The most common mistake with experts is that they do not always get the right people to advise them. To be an expert in one place does not mean that the same principle of expertise applies to a different society. The chicken, a principal ingredient in our English engineer's recipe, may be the same as the one used by the Chinese cook. The spices and cooking utensils can vary from one place to another.

Another problem faced by experts is pity for those who do not have the same lifestyle as they do. Once during a dinner at someone's house, a lady who was just returning from a mission saw that I was African. She came over and started to entertain me with her recent mission.

She had visited some villages where she found children who, she described, were left to themselves and nobody was around to attend to them or feed them. The parents, she added, had gone to look for food. "They had this miserable look on their faces," she said. "They are likely to have problems when they grow up because nobody seems to care for them."

Even professional psychologists would not be able to label these poor children problem prone in one visit. I asked the woman if she searched the whole village and really found nobody the children could report to in case of trouble. There is usually someone in the village looking after them. It is sometimes an old person unable to stay outside due to the heat, or an older child. Because older children have to attend school nowadays, parents cannot take the young ones with them to where they work to gather food. That is why the ones who cannot be wrapped on the backs can stay with someone else in the village. I tried to convince the lady about the parents' confidence in leaving the children in the village. There is loneliness on the children's faces but they know that their parents will come home with food to feed them in the evening. Especially in these villages, no one would consider harming or kidnapping a child.

A second example where the exported expertise does not work concerns two major fields of human life: family planning and nutrition. The UN is not the only system concerned about helping Third World countries to reduce the global population so that the few who are born can lead a decent, standardised life. If the industrialised countries reach a mean of one to two children, why can't the Third World? There are UN, bilateral, and non-governmental programmes which go on the crusade to give people the already-made miraculous products used in Western countries to limit world population.

To earn the trust of any particular culture, especially when sexual behaviour is concerned, one needs more than pamphlets describing or showing genitals. It is better to involve local people who could relate to their own customs. No one is too illiterate to know how two individuals can enjoy sex. Otherwise there would not be special terms in all societies to describe male and female parts of the body. Different cultures have different ways to show affectionate gestures and how to live love.

One thing I have noticed since living in the West is how, during conversations, one cannot describe one's own traditions if a Westerner had lived in one's country. The expert would want to say more, as if he or she was born there. The majority of them become trained anthropologists overnight.

Let us talk about family planning. There is not a single couple in the world who does not feel the weight of having to feed so many mouths, especially when the food is scarce. The first thing people who want to limit child-birth, could do is to look into reasons why traditionally people used to have so many children in some societies.

The root of the problem is showing people that things have changed. With proper medical care and proper diet, the few children one couple bears can make it to old age.

For those who used to depend on children's help, with these latter going to school, they become more of an expense than an asset. To limit the number of children one couple can have, because that has become a norm in many countries, is to favour the preferences of what sex a couple could choose to keep. This attitude has become a major problem in countries where boys are favoured over girls, such as in some Asian countries.

I do not think those who made up the policy of trying to finance or introduce family planning theory looked into this cultural obstacle. I hope it is not too late to reverse the trend, because girls are human beings and need to be protected. It is suggested in an article published in *Newsweek* in 1995 that the male infants will need females to marry so as to perpetuate the human race. I do not mean that the girl's role in society is just to reproduce. Test-tube babies are produced but they still need a woman's womb in which to develop.

The family planning crusade is a good thing. It will need some time because people's mentality takes a long time to change. For it to bear fruit, it should be a package including: a) educational training; b) economic development; c) social and cultural understanding. Men and women should be talked to together. The same principle should also apply to the teaching of how AIDS can be avoided.

As far as malnutrition is concerned, there are different causes. There are well-qualified experts in this field, especially the paramedic teams. The following observation is for the purpose of clarity.

Malnutrition can be present in societies where there is an abundance of food. This is the case in the most industrialised and powerful country, Uncle Sam's, the United States of America. We used to think that being big was a synonym of being healthy. People are discovering that it is not so nowadays. It just means that people are consuming too much to just fill their tummies. Sometimes the diet is not very well balanced.

It is about this balance in diet that I want to talk. Before AIDS, many people who looked skinny were suspected of being undernourished. There are established criteria, of course, according to medical principles. In many Third World countries there are places where there is plenty of food. The major problem sometimes consists in eating the same staple food with no variation. This can have an impact on the weight.

A well-balanced diet programme could be incorporated into the teaching. This would be attended to by trained local people with a minimum cost rather than the most costly seminars undertaken on an international level. The trainers know what the region produces. They also know people's eating habits and taboos. Eating habits are ascribed and cultural, not innate.

A second source of malnutrition is registered in regions wrecked by wars. People flee their homeland and have to be camped where they have no immediate means to feed themselves. In most cases many UN, humanitarian and non-governmental organizations, bring in some emergency aid while the belligerents try to find a solution to the refugee problems.

When one talks about refugees and starvation, most of us who were already adults in the Seventies and Eighties still remember the photos of starving Ethiopians on front pages of newspapers. There could still be famine, malnutrition, fighting in Ethiopia but whatever happened to give back at least the pride to that African nation should be repeated somewhere else.

A third source of famine and malnutrition is drought. Nature is capricious. Some agencies bring food to those areas affected by drought. As in the above situation (war zones), the food solution is always short-lived. People fleeing their land for one reason or another would find a balanced diet for a while. What happens when they return to where they fled? The land may no longer be suitable for cultivation.

Nowadays there are some Third World countries where the staple food can no longer be produced in large quantities due to diseases. That is the case with manioc (cassava, yucca). It is largely consumed in rural areas. Not only does the root rot in the soil but also the soaking method and number of days to dilute the cyanide (which is a poison) has been reduced. This is crippling people. The problem is aggravated by lack of protein intake.

This is not an epidemic for many governments, nor is it a priority to start seeking international aid. It is a big problem in regions where women and children are the major victims. It affects the economy and survival of the community. The most interesting aspect is that government officials are not directly concerned, as is the case with AIDS. They eat very good food and do not drink polluted national water. They can easily buy and consume imported goods.

The preceding examples are of no big importance when one looks at what is going on around the world. There is a lot being done to alleviate the human suffering at the UN and bilateral levels.

It took many years for the World Health Organization (WHO) to declare that the world was free of smallpox. It is a UN specialised agency. The organization did not need to build huge health plants around the world to convince people that smallpox was a dangerous virus which killed and deformed the survivor's skin. What is important is that the message to vaccinate people travelled even to the remotest village. I received my vaccine and my village had no road.

Another UN agency has been receiving positive feedback, the United Nations Children's Fund (UNICEF). Its campaign on immunising children at a certain age has been very well received around the world, regardless of cultural barriers. People need sound information to be convinced. It takes time, patience and understanding. It also took the western hemisphere a long time to acquire the technology and standard of life that its population is enjoying now.

A peaceful settlement that led to independence in which the UN can take full pride is the Namibia case. Elections were conducted in due form in Cambodia as well as a few other countries such as Angola and El Salvador. For this to be achieved, the organization needs the approval of the Security Council of the UN which is a very political institution. This also shows that when people are willing to help and unite, things can change and happen for better or worse.

Why did the author of this manuscript choose to talk about grassroots programmes? For any revolution in society to have strong roots so that the results can have long-lasting effects, it should involve rural populations. In many Third World countries, the majority of people live in rural areas. This argument alone does not suffice because the majority who crowd the urban slums are also poor.

The reasons are many but one can cite a few: A) There are budget cuts in the UN system to maintain not only expensive and gigantic projects but also expensive staff members. Most of them are expatriates. While the experts are needed in some cases, sometimes there are too many whose duties overlap. B) It is expensive to purchase land in big cities if some pilot projects are supposed to be implemented, such as in the case of experimental food programmes. As stated before, some countries are encountering virus problems in producing local food. C) Local staff members, if trained, could do the work, advise their compatriots and cost less because they do not usually receive post adjustment salaries. D) Both men and women should be trained, because regardless of what women do, many of them still care about society and can acquire some skills to improve their ways of living.

Many people will think the above statements are utopian. Those who work with UNICEF and have succeeded in small-scale projects could prove their validity, as well as those who have financed small bilateral projects. There is much waste in the many huge programmes which consume lots of funds. A few projects tend to repeat the ones already in existence without any decent evaluation.

Why not try to send a few bean seeds to some places where there is no war and the food is scarce? The food from the West already made for consumption does not help the people in remote places. It is selling them what is called "roasted peanuts which do not grow." As states a more widely used proverb, "to give fish to someone is to feed her or him for one day. To teach her or him how to fish is to feed her or him for a lifetime."

The biggest disadvantage of sending food subsidies is that people become too dependent and produce less of their staple food which they can buy at a cheaper price. We do not have to be trained economists to evaluate the impact of this type of trading. If the majority of people in many Third World countries live in rural areas, it means many of them do not have paid jobs. If they can cultivate the local produce at least they can feed themselves even, if their diet is not balanced, and if they can sell what they produce, all the better to earn some income. This income will allow people to seek better medical treatment and pay for children's school fees. Many governments in Third World countries do not provide free medical care or schooling for their citizens.

It has been medically proven that healthy mothers-to-be who have a good diet during pregnancy are less likely to bear underweight babies at birth. While food is available in industrialised countries, meaning that people mainly need money to buy it, it is not the same in less developed ones. Pregnant women have to look for their food as well as anybody else. Henceforth, helping them produce their food with less energy, such as shortening the distance to find it, could benefit everyone in the community. Let us face it, we all know that women are the major food providers where paid jobs are non-existent, which is the case in many rural areas.

The transfer of technology, from the North to the South, even on a basic level, is a utopian dream *per se*. It would be useful for the Southern hemisphere to collaborate. The most technologically advanced nations could share the basic components of their tools with others. Industrialised countries do not always carry out financial trading among themselves.

Each country produces different kinds of goods. The illustration in this case can be taken from any African country. This continent is the one where colonialism has planted its strongest roots. The choice is amplified by the simple fact that Africa is economically being wiped out of the international context. It does not mean that the continent does not have any economic potential. It produces bananas, cacao, coffee and tea, all consumable goods which the Western societies enjoy on a daily basis. There are also many minerals that come from this continent which we shall not enumerate.

The following example will illustrate how Africa could best use some products from its own countries.

Once on a mission in Liberia, people were bringing large basins full of live and smoked fish to the hotel. We could not buy it because the hotel was providing our meals. At the market, there were lots of fruit. Liberia is spoiled by nature, one could say. I was looking for a special kind of mango, called in West Africa, pineapple mango. It was only as a whim and for nostalgic reasons. There was no pineapple mango at the market, at least the one I went to.

Back at the hotel, while chatting with the nationals, I teased them about how and why were they letting the fish rot instead of trading it with Burkina Faso. This latter could send them juicy pineapple mangoes in exchange. They nicely told me that they had no commercial ties with Burkina. Liberia, being one of the oldest independent African states it had no special trading partner. It is mainly populated by Black Americans who wanted to create their African nation. The natives kept pointing out that the newcomers took everything over. They were completely in charge. It was fun to talk with them. One can always learn something new. Nobody knew that in a few months the president would be killed.

A month later, I was sent to Burkina Faso on another mission, the country where I could devour the juicy pineapple mangoes. Alas! it was not the season. That did not prevent me from bringing up the subject of exchanging consumable goods with other countries while talking to the Burkinabè. Fish is very expensive in Burkina Faso while mangoes are plentiful. It was easier to discuss with the Liberians than the Burkinabè. Anyway the message got through. I told them that I lived in France and saw at the Ferney-Voltaire market the sign for “mangues du Burkina Faso, pays du soleil”. Why couldn’t they trade them with Liberia for fish? One has to be very diplomatic on some subjects, because people are easily insulted. The answer was identical to the one in Liberia. The difference here was that France has the trading rights with Burkina Faso. Burkina also sells string beans to France. No problem there because many African countries will not even buy string beans. The staple food in many countries is *fufu* (cooked dough made out of pounded cassava, yam or banana plantains), we would rather have it with a gluey sauce made out of fish or meat with a little okra sauce added to it.

Back in Geneva, the idea of finding out more about the exchange of goods among developing countries lingered on for a long time. Finally I addressed the question to some people. The answer was not very different from the people in the field even if it had become more sophisticated. A few people said there was a lot of bureaucracy in Africa. Politicians did not have enough time or qualified personnel to deal with such questions. One person even told me he had started something like that but had no support and had to give up. Another pointed out the language barriers.

The reason for these illustrations is not to suggest that the United Nations should step in to impose common sense among nations. It shows that societies classified as helpless are not so helpless. Sometimes they are strangled by rules beyond their control. To help them on a smaller scale would give them more dignity and control over their lives.

Those who have been to and lived in some Third World countries know how transport can be a real nightmare for the nationals. Their ingenuity impresses many people. When technology is adapted to people's needs, it can be a boon even to those who cannot read or write.

In one West African country, the use of motorcycles is very common. Those who work can even buy the most sophisticated models. What is fascinating is how people use them. They are used for personal transport as well as the transport of relatives and even merchandise. The proudest users are women. The majority of them purchase their own, which makes them independent.

These *mobilettes* consume very little petrol compared to cars and are easily repaired locally. The mechanics are not university or high school graduates.

While still a graduate student at an American university in the States, I travelled to that country for a few weeks. The experience was so enriching I wanted to share my discovery with other students in our international market management class. The professor was Swedish. The Americans were behind the Japanese in the early Eighties because Japanese products sold better overseas than American ones.

In Third World countries where manufacturing plants were scarce, people could not use American-made machines. They were either too big, especially cars, which also had a high fuel consumption, or one needed a transformer to adapt to the current. The transformer weighed and also cost a lot of money to purchase.

The students were very defensive about the new technology. They thought that it was up to the nationals to make up their minds. Since we had to analyse advertising techniques on how to export products overseas, the professor asked us to put our methods in writing. He added that our purpose was to find some trading partners and sell our ideas. Finally I told him that we had no right to impose our methods on others. He was just provoking students, he said. At the end he told us that we had a choice between behavioural management and the course we were in. He did not think that those who wanted to make a profit would subscribe to the former.

The whole chapter on expertise is to show how far the experts can go and the gaps that remain between expectations and realities. The United Nations is not a political institution or a profit-making one *per se*. It represents a special hope for many developing countries. The United Nations Development Programme (UNDP) has offices in many parts of the world. It works closely with some governments. It could, with the help of UN personnel, find a few ways to carry out more small-scale projects to benefit people in the most remote areas. Unfortunately, many UN organizations compete and duplicate programmes.

In general, aid packages and financial loans are like drugs that a patient takes knowing the possibility of side-effects. How many times have the International Monetary Fund (IMF) and the World Bank lent money to poor countries? In many cases some of them cannot even pay back the accumulated interest. In countries where devaluation is forced by these institutions which pretend to bring some economic balance, the results are very often disastrous for the majority of the population. They are the ones who pay the highest price even if they consume locally grown food.

One African country fought several times to avoid the devaluation suggestion. That was Tanzania under President Nyerere's rule. He finally could not win. The leaders and policy-makers of these institutions convince people that those austerity measures are the solution to economic stagnation. Poor people in countries where these measures failed do not get any feedback. Thank God there are evaluations to show the policy - and decision-makers that the real solution does not lie in lending money alone.

Now the World Bank is making small loans available to women's projects as well as to others on individual initiatives where there is credibility for generating income and work.

It is not always easy to explain or implement one's ideas when one follows them within a bureaucratic framework. Unfortunately, the United Nations is sometimes victim of the behaviour of its members and immediate employers. Would the organization fare better if its employees had a little more sympathy and contact with the people they are supposed to serve?

The UN has set a few priorities for the 21st Century: Health for All, No More Hunger, Good Drinking Water, to name a few. However, the governments operate in the same old way: negotiating priorities with the UN and formulating development projects. Not a long time ago, there was a commentary in a local newspaper in favour of maintaining development projects to poor countries. The article stated that one Swiss franc invested in a development project in a poor country brings four francs back to Switzerland. If one were to reverse the equation, would the poor country say the same?

Some Western countries dump expired drugs or those no longer in use in developed countries on the markets of Third World, and especially African, countries. The UN is not the world's policeman to prevent such abuses. However, it could, through its specialized agencies, reach the most disadvantaged groups, the rural populations, and arm them with basic technology as it is doing in the Sahelian countries (such as Burkina, Faso, Mali, Niger to name a few) with improved woodstoves and cooking methods programmes.

There is a very good book which the author suggests that the UN library acquire. It is called *Horton Hears a Who* by Dr. Seuss. A big elephant is ridiculed carrying around this small clover leaf, claiming it is full of small people. Horton never gives up until the smallest voice is heard to save the whole group.

Horton keeps on repeating, "A person is a person, no matter how small." It is these smallest voices living in the most remote areas which could change the outcome for the poorest countries.